The City-Women

CMUP Drama
Wendy Arons, Series Editor

The City-Women

Mallorie Sievert

Carnegie Mellon University Press
Pittsburgh 2026

Book design by Connie Amoroso

Library of Congress Control Number 2026937117
ISBN 978-0-88748-748-4

Printed and bound in the United States of America

10 9 8 7 6 5 4 3 2 1

The City-Women

CHARACTERS

ANA: A teenage girl. A novice nun. Vastly spiritual with a core of fire and a natural aversion to rules and structure. Latine/BIPOC (indigenous preferred).

TERESA: A teenage girl. A novice nun. A true bride of Christ in a traditional sense. A truly humble heart and a quiet strength, and effortlessly funny in an understated way. Latine/any race.

NICOLASA: 40s–50s woman. The Prioress of the convent. A very hard, strict exterior, but has a soft spot for Ana. Latine/any race.

MARÍA: A teenage girl. An initiate nun. Very smart, cunning, and calculated. Life is a chess game, and she is always three steps ahead of everyone else. Latine/any race.

All four characters should be ethnically Latine if possible, and Ana must be BIPOC (ideally indigenous), while the other three characters can be any race. Colorism and classism inform the character relationships throughout this script: while never explicitly stated, the character of Ana is implied to be of indigenous/not white origin, while the other three characters are implied to be of Spanish colonial origin from Arequipa, Peru.

SETTING

The Santa Catalina Monastery in Arequipa, Peru.

TIME

Seventeenth century CE.

AUTHOR'S NOTE

A slash (/) is used to indicate an interruption.

Additionally, as is the tradition in theatrical works, punctuation marks are used as dynamic marks that indicate the manner of speech of the character, disregarding classic grammar rules. The punctuation should be used as a tool to inform an actor's interpretation of the character and the line.

Finally, this play was written for a contemporary English-speaking audience, with the setting and time period being merely a device to tell what is, at its core, a universal love story. The modernized English as opposed to period accurate Spanish dialogue is an intentional stylistic choice to bring this story to an audience that feels, thinks, and loves in the same manner as characters that would otherwise be inaccessible to them.

ACT I

SCENE 1

(The chapel. The nuns are praying the Rosary aloud, led by Madre Nicolasa, the Prioress of the monastery. The Rosary can be translated into English for a primarily English speaking audience.)

NICOLASA

Dios te salve, María, Llena eres de gracia, el Señor es contigo. Bendita tú eres entre todas las mujeres, y bendito es el fruto de tu vientre, Jesús.

ALL

Santa María, Madre de Dios, ruega por nosotros, pecadores, ahora y en la hora de nuestra muerte, Amén.

NICOLASA

Gloria al Padre, al Hijo y al Espíritu Santo.

ALL

Como era en el principio, ahora y siempre, por los siglos de los siglos, Amén.

NICOLASA

Oh Jesús mío, perdona nuestros pecados.

ALL

Líbranos del fuego del infierno, lleva al cielo a todas las almas, especialmente a las más necesitadas de tu misericordia.

NICOLASA

El Cuarto Misterio Doloroso: El Traslado—

(Suddenly, the door flies open, and Ana rushes in, a bit frazzled, habit not on properly. The nuns all look up at her, disturbed.)

Sor Ana, please take a seat. There is no need to be disruptive. El Cuarto Misterio Doloroso: El Traslado de la Cruz.

(Ana heads to the back of the chapel and kneels next to Teresa. The other nuns continue the Rosary underneath the following scene.)

TERESA

(Whispering) Where were you last night?!

ANA

I fell asleep in the rejas.

TERESA

What?!

ANA

The vendor who brought the shipment of beans I picked up for Sor Luisa yesterday is a musician, he plays in the plaza. I bribed him and his brothers to come to the rejas last night and play for me.

TERESA

You're lucky you only share a room with me.

ANA

(Smiles) I am.

TERESA

How did you bribe him?

ANA

I gave him my tin of chocolate.

TERESA

(Offended) Ana!

ANA

I don't even like chocolate!

TERESA

Yeah, but *I* do!

(Ana smiles at her. One of the other nuns shoots them a look, and they quickly jump right back into the Rosary with the rest of the nuns. Ana smiles to herself, then joins in as well. They say a few beads, then break off into conversation once again.)

ANA

(Whispering to Teresa again) The charango player played so beautifully, Teresa. I wish I'd had the courage to sing with them but I was too scared. I'd never heard music like that before. It had so much life.

TERESA

I can't believe you met a bunch of street musicians in the rejas. That's so dangerous.

ANA

How? There were two walls of grates between us, I could barely even see them.

TERESA

(Indignant) Still.

(Ana smiles at her again.)

What?

ANA

Nothing.

TERESA

You're—

ANA

Wow, I can't believe you're not paying attention to the Rosary. What a bad nun, Tere.

(Teresa makes a face at her. Ana smiles. They both join back into the Rosary for the ending.)

NICOLASA

Ruega por nosotros, Santa Madre de Dios.

ALL

Para que seamos dignos de alcanzar las promesas de Nuestro Señor Jesucristo.

NICOLASA

Oh Dios, cuyo Unigénito Hijo con su vida, muerte y resurrección, ha comprado para nosotros la recompensa de la vida eterna, concédenos, te rogamos, que, al meditar los Misterios del Más Santo Rosario de la Bienaventurada Virgen María, imitemos lo que contienen y obtengamos lo que promete, por el mismo Cristo nuestro Señor. Amén.

ALL

Amén.

(All the nuns begin to pack up their things and leave.)

ANA

Why are you in such a hurry?

TERESA

I have to embroider fifteen new altar cloths today. I was too worried about where you were to get anything started last night, so thanks a lot.

ANA

Oh, I'm sorry.

NICOLASA

(Calling from across the room) Sor Ana!

ANA

(To Teresa) Mother calls.

TERESA

(Leaving) Bye. See you later.

ANA

I'm sorry about the cloths.

(She goes. Ana goes to Nicolasa.)

Madre Nicolasa.

NICOLASA

What happened? Why were you late?

ANA

I overslept. I'm sorry Prioress.

NICOLASA

Why didn't Sor Teresa wake you?

(Silence. Nicolasa chooses not to pry further.)

NICOLASA

Don't let it happen again.

ANA

(With sudden causality) Nica, I had such a strange dream last night.

NICOLASA

You cannot call me Nica anymore, Sor Ana, you are grown now.

ANA

Whatever.

NICOLASA

You are a novice nun, not my protégé, not my niña.

ANA

(Impatiently) Okay! (with emphasis) *Madre Nicolasa,* last night I had a dream I don't understand, but it really scared me. I dreamed that I was flying, that my soul left my body and flew up and out of my room, and I was flying over the whole city, and then the whole world, and then I flew up into space, and everything was so tiny beneath me. I felt so warm and light all of a sudden, like nothing really mattered all that much anyway, and then I SWEAR I felt a presence over my shoulder, like someone was right behind me, watching it all from that distance too, and I felt His hand touch my shoulder.

And then I was back.

NICOLASA

In your bed?

ANA

In my body.

(Nicolasa gives her a look.)

ANA

Which was totally in my bed.

NICOLASA

It's an interesting dream, Anita.

ANA

(Smirking) Anita?

NICOLASA

Sor Ana.

(Ana smiles at her precociously.)

Write your dreams down, Ana. God will make them clear to you.

ANA

Thank you, Madre Nicolasa.

NICOLASA

Now get going, I'm sure you have things to do. I know I do. Oh! And Ana, will you stop by my office today after Mass? I have something I'd like to speak to you about.

ANA

Of course.

NICOLASA

You know your music?

ANA

Yes, Nica.

NICOLASA

I'm just making sure! I'm sure you didn't oversleep because you were up late last night reviewing Von Bingen's lyrics—

ANA

Have I ever not known the songs?

NICOLASA

Okay, okay! Scram, get going!

ANA

I want to stay and pray for a minute.

NICOLASA

Don't be long.

ANA

Yeah, yeah, bye!

(They wave each other off dismissively with the casualty of two people who know each other well and love each other deeply, and Nicolasa goes. Ana kneels right in front of the altar and closes her eyes. After a moment, a white light shines directly above her. She opens her eyes and smiles, turning her face to the light. Then, she stands up and begins to dance hypnotically, completely enraptured by the boundless joy she feels.)

SCENE 2

(Teresa sits on the floor in the middle of the novices' cloister, leaning against an orange tree. She's embroidering, lost in thought. Ana sees her and watches from behind. After a moment, she steps forward and Teresa notices her, startled.)

TERESA

Oh gosh, how long have you been lurking?

ANA

I like watching you. It's hypnotic.

TERESA

Don't you have places to be?

ANA

I'd rather be here with you.

(Teresa smiles and shakes her head.)

How do you stay focused all day? I think I would go crazy.

TERESA

Thank God you have other talents.

ANA

He knows I don't do well sitting still for long periods of time.

TERESA

You chose the perfect vocation for that. Nuns are famous for their exciting lifestyles.

ANA

(Laughing) I've found my ways. Besides, I never really had a choice. I was never going to do anything else.

(Beat.)

TERESA

Every stitch is a prayer.

ANA

What?

TERESA

You asked how I stay focused. I'm not just embroidering. I'm always praying. With everything I do.

(The light flashes white above. Ana turns her face to it and smiles.)

ANA

I know what you mean.

TERESA

Do you want to try?

ANA

I have. I'm awful at it. Like you said, thank God I have other talents. I would be absolutely useless here otherwise.

TERESA

Come sit. I'll help you.

ANA

I'm going to mess up all your work.

TERESA

It's fine, I can fix it.

(Begrudgingly, Ana sits with Teresa and takes the altar cloth from her hands.)

TERESA

(Guiding her) Put it through here.

(Ana slowly pierces the cloth with the needle. She tries to pull it out the other end, but it gets stuck.)

ANA

Oh no–

TERESA

It's okay, you just have to do it gently, like–(taking Ana's hands in her own and guiding her)–like this. You're just leading the needle, you're not forcing it. Like it's water. Now again, through here.

(Ana pierces the cloth again, making another stitch, Teresa's hands guiding hers the whole way.)

Good.

(Another stitch.)

It's like a prayer, you see? The repetition of it, the humility in it. Right here.

(Another stitch.)

ANA

Tere–

TERESA

You're doing good.

(Another stitch. Another stitch.)

Do you feel it? The peace?

ANA

(Bluntly) No.

TERESA

(Laughing) Ana!

ANA

I can't lie to you Tere, this sucks. Like this is awful.

TERESA

(Playfully) Just give it back to me. I have to undo your stitches anyway.

ANA

So you were lying to me too?

(Teresa smiles at her precociously and begins to undo her stitches.)

It's singing for me.

TERESA

What?

ANA

My prayer.

TERESA

Your turn, then. Show me, sing something, one of the songs for Mass today.

ANA

(Amused) I can't, I don't know them yet.

TERESA

Oh my goodness. Please go learn them.

ANA

I'll see you at dinner?

TERESA

Go!

(Ana laughs and runs out of the courtyard. Teresa smiles after her, then returns to her stitches.)

SCENE 3

(Nicolasa's office after Mass.)

NICOLASA

Mass today was special, was it not?

ANA

It was.

NICOLASA

I could hear it in your voice. You always sound beautiful, but today. . . .

ANA

I felt not only God's presence, Nica, but every woman who has come before me, all the unnamed women whose stories were eclipsed by those of John and Simon Peter and Matthew and Paul—

NICOLASA

Eclipsed? Those are the fathers of our church—

ANA

No, I know. I just sometimes wonder about the mothers, that's all.

(Beat.)

NICOLASA

There is nothing to wonder about, mija. The Bible tells us everything we need to know. The Church tells us everything we need to know.

ANA

You're right.

NICOLASA

Ana, we have several new girls coming later today and throughout this week hoping to begin their journey as initiates—

ANA

Really? The last new girl was—

NICOLASA

It's been a while, I know. Prioress Yolanda . . . she was doing her best, but she was so old, there has been a lot I've needed to catch up on in these past few months. Anyway, I wanted to talk to you about these new initiates because I need your help, mija.

ANA

Show them around, be a good example, yeah yeah I got it.

NICOLASA

Yes *and*. Yes, all of those things, but . . . I received another letter from the Bishop today. In my new position I hear more than I would care to know . . . our world is changing, and the Bishop is putting a lot of pressure on us to really tighten up, crack down on the rules, show our strength.

ANA

What do you mean?

NICOLASA

There are things happening in Europe. Things you don't need to worry about. There are some people that don't believe in the Catholic Church anymore, and they're turning away in waves and creating their own versions of Christianity.

ANA

What?!

NICOLASA

We are lucky to be here, with an ocean—and a very Catholic king—to protect us, but across New Spain we're being told to fortify.

ANA

Are they not afraid for their souls?

NICOLASA

They're not even afraid for their children's. Some of these new sects believe you should *choose* when to be baptized; they're refusing to baptize their children and rather waiting for them to come of age to choose for themselves.

ANA

(Suddenly remembering) I had a dream that I baptized myself. I baptized myself in a tank full of seals, they were trying to kill me. And when God saw me He was so pleased that He set fire to the water and killed every last one of them. I was untouched.

NICOLASA

(Excited) Perhaps God was sending you a vision of the Lake of Fire. Only further proof that we must hold true to our faith.

ANA

Maybe.

NICOLASA

I need your help, Ana, because some of these new girls may come from quite affluent families, families who would be privy to what's going on, and you will be spending much more time with them than I will. Yes, I want you to show them around, be a good example, all of those things, but I also need you to be a strong beacon of our faith and a soldier for our Church. If you hear talk, anything that might imply that the Church does not hold the power it used to, shut it down. We mustn't show weakness, give them any reason to doubt the Bishop's power, and we must maintain the sanctity of the cloister for the rest of our sisters. I need you to be a Shepherd, mija. Help me guide this flock.

ANA

A fisher of men.

NICOLASA

(Smiling) Of women.

ANA

I bet it's the *men* coming up with these crazy ideas.

NICOLASA

(Smiling beside herself) Probably.

ANA

The men in the Bible are all so hotheaded. The Apostles were always arguing about something.

NICOLASA

You're not wrong.

ANA

They should've just put María Magdalena in charge. She always seemed to know what was going on.

NICOLASA

Okay, okay, (waving her away) off to bed. Thank you for your help, mija. I always know I can trust you. I am very proud of the woman you have become.

ANA

Thank you.

NICOLASA

Even if you show up late to the Rosary.

ANA

Aaaaand you ruined it. (Leaving) Love you, Nica!

NICOLASA

(Amused) Goodbye.

(Ana leaves.)

(Under her breath) I love you too.

SCENE 4

(It's nighttime. The sisters are all heading to bed soon. Teresa is sitting in their cell, embroidering on the sleeve of one of Ana's habits. Ana is heard humming in the hall, and Teresa panics and looks for a place to hide the habit, but is too late: Ana has entered.)

TERESA

Stop, stop, wait! Don't look!

ANA

What?

TERESA

Close your eyes!

(Ana closes her eyes and freezes. Beat. Teresa is furiously trying to finish her embroidery.)

ANA

Can I open my eyes now?

TERESA

No!

(Ana hesitates for a moment, and then puts her arms out and attempts to find her bed blindly. She is not very successful.)

What are you doing?

ANA

What are *you* doing?! I'm just trying to find my stuff.

(Teresa smiles for a moment, then gets up and guides Ana to her bed. Ana sits.)

ANA

Can I open my eyes now?

TERESA

One second, I'm almost finished . . . okay. . . .

(Teresa goes and puts the habit in Ana's lap and sits down next to her.)

TERESA

. . . and open!

(Ana opens her eyes and looks at the habit, confused.)

ANA

It's a habit.

TERESA

It's your habit. And look (she opens one of the sleeves and reveals the embroidery.)

ANA

(Delighted) It's a heart!

TERESA

It's a heart!

ANA

You embroidered a heart in my sleeve?

TERESA

Do you like it?

ANA

I love it.

TERESA

Just don't tell anyone. (Ana laughs) I thought you might want something to set yours apart so you don't keep grabbing the wrong one from laundry.

ANA

It's not my fault they all look the same!

TERESA

(Laughing) like the time–

ANA

(Embarrassed) Stoooop!

TERESA

(Imitating her flapping long sleeves) You looked like a little baby with your sleeves flapping–

ANA

Trust me, Nica never let me hear the end of that one.

(Teresa now starts to undress so she can change into her nightgown. She faces away from Ana and unties her habit, and slips it off. She's standing in just her undergarments as she reaches for her nightgown in the drawer. Ana watches her for a moment, then averts her eyes, looking anywhere else. Teresa, now in her nightgown, shivers, and crawls under the covers of her bed.)

TERESA

It's getting colder out. I might have to get my winter habit out soon.

ANA

Cold?! It's barely autumn!

TERESA

It's *cold*!

(Suddenly, a young nun walks past their room and looks in the open door, then keeps walking. Ana and Teresa look at each other quizzically.)

TERESA

Who was that?

ANA

I don't know.

(The nun walks back the other way.)

ANA

(Calling after her) Hey! Girl!

(María appears again in the doorway. She is about the same age as the other girls, maybe a year or two younger. She's wearing initiate clothing.)

MARÍA

Hi, sorry, I'm just a little lost.

TERESA

(Recognition hitting her) María?

MARÍA

. . . Teresa Martín?

TERESA

It's just Sor Teresa now.

MARÍA

Tesa! I haven't seen you in years!

TERESA

Well I've been here since I was ten.

MARÍA

I'm so envious. I just got here this morning. I just can't seem to remember how to get back to my room, it's like a maze in here.

ANA

Initiates are directly across the cloister.

TERESA

Oh! Ana, this is María. We played together as girls. Our fathers are friends.

MARÍA

You sang at Mass this evening!

ANA

I did.

MARÍA

You have a beautiful voice.

ANA

Thank you.

TERESA

What brings you here, María?

MARÍA

I'm sorry, I didn't mean to lurk, I just couldn't find my room—

TERESA

I mean here, to the monastery. I thought you were going to marry.

MARÍA

Oh. I was going to. I was promised and everything, but my father and I realized that this was my true vocation. I just knew in my heart that this was where I belonged. David was a bit of a bore, anyway. He and his family weren't very happy with this choice, but I told them that if they tried to force me to marry against God's will, I would never lie with him, and if he tried to force himself upon me, I would take out my own womb with a kitchen knife to ensure that I would never bring him an heir and to punish myself for committing the sin of the body.

(Beat.)

(With a smile) So eventually they relented and allowed me to come here.

TERESA

Wow.

MARÍA

(To Ana) Where did you say my room would be again?

ANA

Across the cloister. On the other side of the crosses.

MARÍA

Thank you!

(She goes and hugs Teresa.)

It's so good to see you, Tesa! Now we're *actually* sisters!

(María goes. A moment of silence.)

ANA

Jesus Christ.

TERESA

(Reprimanding her) Ana!

ANA

(Gesturing vaguely at the sky as though apologizing to a parent she's very comfortable with) Sorry.

(Beat.)

Nicolasa's gonna love her.

SCENE 5

(Dinner. Teresa and Ana sit together at a table, mid conversation. Teresa is stressed, and Ana is comforting her.)

ANA

You'll get it done. You always do.

TERESA

I just probably won't sleep much tonight.

ANA

I'll stay up with you.

(Teresa smiles at her as María walks up to their table with a plate of food and sits.)

MARÍA

Tesa! I've missed you, I haven't seen you in days!

ANA

We all have the same schedule.

MARÍA

(Still addressing Teresa) I know, but you're always sitting with Ana! I've missed you!

ANA

(Annoyed) I'm gonna go get some more beans. Tere, you want any?

TERESA

(Handing Ana her plate) Oh sure, thank you!

(Ana gets up and leaves. María watches her go.)

MARÍA

What is up with her and the prioress? After every service today she hung back and talked to her, and I've even seen them . . . hug. But Prioress Nicolasa seems to be very strict with everyone else.

TERESA

Oh. It's complicated.

MARÍA

Complicated how?

TERESA

Ana . . . has a bit of a different past.

MARÍA

Is she related to the prioress?

TERESA

No, not really.

MARÍA

Why are you being so vague?

TERESA

I don't know, it's Ana's life. I don't want to gossip about it.

MARÍA

It's not gossip, I just want to know the monastery's history.

(Beat.)

I'm sorry, I didn't mean to make you uncomfortable! Really, Tesa, I just wanted to know a little more about my new home. I just still feel like such an outsider. I really am sorry, I shouldn't have asked–

TERESA

No, no, it's okay.

MARÍA

I'm sorry.

TERESA

Don't be sorry, you're right, most people here know anyway. It's not a secret. Prioress Nicolasa essentially raised Ana.

MARÍA

Oh?

TERESA

Ana's parents left her here when she was a toddler. They just dropped her off in the middle of the night with a note requesting that we employ her as a servant.

MARÍA

A baby?

TERESA

Yeah. I know, it's sad. Well no one really knows why, but Nicolasa decided to take her under her wing, gave her a bed in her own room. Someone eventually discovered Ana could sing—really well—and boom—one way ticket into the sisterhood.

MARÍA

Hm. I knew there was something fishy about her.

TERESA

What do you mean?

MARÍA

Just that she doesn't really seem like you and me, you know?

TERESA

No, I don't really know what you mean—

MARÍA

She doesn't . . . come from where we come from, Tesa.

TERESA

(Sarcastically) Because where we come from is so perfect and idyllic.

(Ana comes back and sits at the table with them.)

MARÍA

It's interesting you bring that up actually: do you remember Luisa la Roja?

TERESA

Yes. Wow, I forgot about her.

MARÍA

Word is that she ran away.

TERESA

What?

MARÍA

She disappeared. And so did her servant. Her female dresser.

ANA

(Genuinely confused) What?

MARÍA

I just always thought there was something a bit *wrong* with her, that's all. I always thought she was a bit touchy when we played, didn't you, Tesa?

TERESA

I don't really remember well. I always liked her. I hope she's okay.

MARÍA

But you're right, bad eggs can come from any batch, even ours. It's just so great to be in a place free from all that, finally. Speaking of, I wanted to be early for Confession today, I should get going. Who'll be in the confessional today, do you know?

TERESA

Padre Bartolomé.

MARÍA

Bartolomé! Named after one of my favorite martyrs! (In awe) Being flayed alive. What a way to go. (Ana nearly chokes on her food) Careful Ana, protect that beautiful voice of yours! Alright, love you girls! See you later! (She goes)

ANA

I can't stand her.

TERESA

She really does mean well.

ANA

Why are you defending her?

TERESA

I don't know I just . . . it's been so long since I've seen anyone from my childhood. I'm just trying to see the best in her, 'cause . . . you know.

ANA

Are you okay?

TERESA

Yeah, I'm fine.

(Ana gives her a look.)

I just . . . I don't know. Seeing María is bringing up a lot of memories. I didn't realize how much I missed home. And I'm happy here, I really am, this is the life I chose, but I don't know. I just miss home sometimes.

(Beat.)

ANA

Can I show you something?

TERESA

What?

ANA

Not now. Tonight. When it gets dark.

TERESA

I have so much work, Ana.

ANA

It'll be so quick! I promise.

(Teresa gives her a look.)

Come on, give the cloths to Nicolasa a day late. Who cares? Aren't you tired of being perfect all the time? I promise it'll be worth it.

SCENE 6

(A rooftop in the monastery. Ana is guiding Teresa up the stairs, Teresa has her eyes closed.)

TERESA

It doesn't seem very safe to have me climbing stairs with my eyes closed, at night.

ANA

Why does the night part matter? You can't see anyway.

TERESA

(Smiling) Why are we always so dramatic with our surprises?

ANA

Sh!

(Ana leads Teresa to the edge of the roof very carefully.)

Okay . . . now open.

(Teresa opens her eyes and gasps. Tears begin to well in her eyes.)

TERESA

It's the whole city.

ANA

I know.

TERESA

It's beautiful.

ANA

Yeah.

TERESA

There's the plaza! I didn't realize we were so close.

ANA

Close enough to hear the music during the day, if you listen really closely.

TERESA

There! That's the road my sisters and I used to . . . that means my house must be. . . . (She draws a path with her finger) There's a light on in the living room.

ANA

Where?

TERESA

That one. Waaay over there, on the other side of the river.

ANA

(Laughing) There's so many houses there, Tere.

TERESA

That one! Right there!

ANA

I don't know which one you're pointing at!

TERESA

Oh well. I know which one it is. How did you find this place?

ANA

I was left alone a lot when I was younger. I explored quite a bit.

TERESA

Thank you. For showing me.

(Ana smiles at her.)

Do you remember where you used to live?

ANA

No.

TERESA

Oh.

ANA

I remember glimpses. I remember we had a yellow kitchen. I remember my mom's hands. I remember my brother bringing me water in bed when I was sick.

TERESA

Oh.

ANA

(Plaintively) I don't remember his name.

TERESA

I'm sorry they don't come.

ANA

Don't be.

TERESA

I am.

ANA

That's not my life anymore.

TERESA

I guess not.

ANA

I wonder what it would be like too, sometimes. If I still lived out there. I like to come up here and imagine it.

TERESA

(Excitedly) I'd want to talk to a *boy* who's not a priest!

ANA

(Amused) Would you really?

TERESA

(Admitting it and laughing) No, not really–

ANA

Me neither!

TERESA

I'm actually okay /I have no interest . . .

ANA

They seem kinda gross!

TERESA

Yeah I don't know why I said that!

(Ana laughs.)

ANA

I'd want to ride a horse.

TERESA

Really? Of all the things you'd do in the real world, you'd ride a horse?

ANA

Yes. Obviously. They're sick as hell.

TERESA

(Laughing) You're crazy.

ANA

Okay, Miss Judgemental, what would *you* do then?

TERESA

(Thoughtfully) I would love to be in love.

ANA

(Teasing) Oh, you gave a real answer.

TERESA

I would! My parents love each other so much. They can't touch *me*, but once a year through the gaps in the rejas I see them grasping at each others' hands like they're trying to drink each other in, and that love is so thick, it feels so palpable. . . . I see that, and I *feel* it in the air, and I am suddenly so lonely.

(Ana looks at Teresa, unreadable.)

What?

ANA

Nothing.

(Beat. Teresa looks out at the city. Ana's gaze stays fixed on Teresa, not moving.)

TERESA

Really Ana, thank you. This is . . . thank you.

(Beat.)

What's your real answer?

ANA

To what?

TERESA

If you lived out there, what would you want to do? If you could do anything?

(Ana thinks for a moment.)

ANA

I'd want to sing in a street band.

TERESA

(Laughing) Really?

ANA

No, I'm completely serious. I hear that charango player in my dreams, Tere. And the pan flute. I didn't know music could sound like that. I wonder what my voice could sound like, if I set it free.

TERESA

Why don't you try it?

ANA

What?

TERESA

Right now. Sing! At the top of your lungs!

ANA

(Smiling) No, I can't.

TERESA

Why not?

ANA

I don't know. I don't know how. I don't want to wake anyone.

TERESA

Oh, right. (Having a realization) Wait, are we allowed to be up here?

ANA

I don't know. Probably not. (Amused) Why, are you worried now?

TERESA

We should probably leave. I don't want to get in trouble.

ANA

(Laughing) Okay, if you say so.

(As they start to leave, Teresa turns back around.)

TERESA

Maybe just a few more minutes.

(Teresa looks out at the city again. Ana smiles, watching her. After a moment Teresa notices.)

TERESA

What?

ANA

Nothing.

TERESA

Okay, we should actually go now. I can't turn in the cloths late *and* be caught trespassing. You've corrupted me, Ana.

ANA

(Laughing) Whatever you say.

TERESA

I say we leave.

(She takes one last peek at the city. Ana laughs and grabs her hand, pulling her away.)

ANA

Come on, Little Miss Perfect.

TERESA

I was leaving! I'm the one who wanted to leave in the first place.

ANA

(Smiling) Okay.

(As they go down the stairs, hand in hand:)

TERESA

Maybe we can come back another time. Just to make sure no one else is trespassing up here.

ANA

(Laughing) Okay.

SCENE 7

(Late evening. In the church, before Mass is to begin. Nicolasa is mid conversation with María.)

NICOLASA

And you've never had formal musical training?

MARÍA

No, ma'am, but I've always been told I am naturally gifted. My father suggested to me earlier today that I see what leadership opportunities—

NICOLASA

Earlier today? You met with him in the rejas? Did I approve this?

MARÍA

Padre Bartolomé sent me.

NICOLASA

These things shouldn't go through him, they should go through me, I oversee all the sisters—

MARÍA

Maybe he assumed that because you are so new it would be better to talk to Padre Bartolomé—

NICOLASA

I'll speak to him about this. Each sister is only allowed an outside visitor once a year.

MARÍA

My father is very close friends with the Bishop, they have a sort of arrangement I believe. He doesn't like to go long without speaking to me—

NICOLASA

Then he shouldn't have sent you to a cloistered convent.

MARÍA

I'm sorry, Madre. I didn't know about the meeting.

NICOLASA

If the Bishop is involved there may not be anything we can do.

MARÍA

So . . . about me singing at Mass?

NICOLASA

Well, you know, we are quite set with our music, Ana has been studying since–

MARÍA

No, no, of course, I would never want to overstep. Is she feeling alright? Shouldn't the cantor be here by now?

NICOLASA

Sor Ana likes to keep me on my toes.

MARÍA

She's certainly unconventional.... May I speak plainly with you, Madre Nicolasa?

NICOLASA

What's bothering you?

MARÍA

Thank goodness I'm as disciplined as I am, but I worry for some of the others.

NICOLASA

What are you implying?

MARÍA

Just that I've noticed that Sor Ana's influence seems to be corrupting some of my contemporaries, the other initiates.

NICOLASA

Ana? No.

MARÍA

I sometimes see her just sitting around, watching the clouds or playing with bugs while the rest of the sisters are working and praying.

NICOLASA

I assure you, Sor María, you do not need to worry about Ana. Focus on yourself, on your own faith life.

MARÍA

It's just difficult when the girls that I live with get upset with me for waking up at dawn to pray the Rosary, or when I'm the only initiate early to Mass because the others are out enjoying the sunshine for as long as possible. It's lonely.

NICOLASA

This can be a lonely life. It's not easy, devoting yourself to Christ. But He will sustain you.

MARÍA

No, I mean it's lonely in the sense that I seem to be alone in my devotion. But I guess they're right, no one seems to take this life seriously anymore. Why would they when there's no punishment for being lazy and no reward for caring?

NICOLASA

The reward is eternal life.

MARÍA

I know that, but I'm not sure the Bishop agrees. I know my father certainly doesn't.

(Just then, Ana walks in. She sees María already in the church, and gives her a look.)

MARÍA

Oh hi Ana! We were just talking about you.

NICOLASA

Really cutting things a bit close these days, aren't you Ana?

ANA

Am I late? I didn't think I was late–

NICOLASA

You know very well what time it is.

ANA

(She decides to brush it off) Nica–(looking at María and catching herself) Madre Nicolasa . . . could I talk to you for a moment?

NICOLASA

What's bothering you?

ANA

I . . .

(Ana glances at María, hoping she'll get the hint that this should be a private conversation. María does not, in fact, get it.)

Well, I had another dream last night. I can't make out what God's trying to tell me.

NICOLASA

You and your dreams.

ANA

(As she speaks, the light begins to glow white above her)
I had a dream that I was my own mother, and I was giving birth to myself. And as I held myself in my own arms, I became the midwife, tending to me the mother and to me the baby. And then suddenly I was *me* me, watching the whole scene from right outside the birthing room, and I somehow knew, down to my soul, that I was barren, or at least that I would not bear, but I could feel the labor pains of me the mother, and it was excruciating, and I could sense that there were hundreds of women—hundreds of people—living in my skin, itching to be seen and remembered. I was all of them.

MARÍA

I used to want kids too, but now I know nothing can sustain you like Christ.

ANA

That's not the point. It's not that straightforward.

MARÍA

Why can't it be? Why can't it just be God testing you and seeing how much you really want this life? Dreaming about anything else is sinful.

ANA

It's funny, but I don't recall asking you to be a part of this conversation.

NICOLASA

(Pointedly) Ana.

ANA

You're reprimanding *me*?

NICOLASA

You know anger is not Godly.

ANA

And hypocrisy is?

NICOLASA

Sor María, could you give us a moment alone, please?

MARÍA

Of course, Sor Nicolasa. I would be happy to. Would I be able to wait by the tabernacle? I love to sit in the presence of Jesus himself as I prepare myself for Mass.

NICOLASA

That is fine.

ANA

(Under her breath) Of course.

MARÍA

(Pointedly ignoring Ana and speaking only to Nicolasa) Thank you. I'll see you at Mass.

(Ana and Nicolasa say nothing as they watch María go. Once she is out of earshot, Nicolasa speaks.)

NICOLASA

Ana, I need you to care more.

ANA

Care more?

NICOLASA

People are watching you, Ana.

ANA

Is this a joke? What do you mean I don't *care*? I care so deeply, I love God more than anyone, you *know* I do—

NICOLASA

I know Ana, but everything you do has an impact on the people around you, and it all reflects back on our monastery and on me as Prioress.

ANA

What happened? Did I do something wrong?

NICOLASA

You're just not doing *enough,* and I need more from you. You are a leader in this monastery, and your sisters look up to you.

ANA

I don't understand–

NICOLASA

I know you don't like her, but you could really learn something from Sor María.

ANA

What? Are you kidding me? She just parades around telling everybody how good of a person she is–

NICOLASA

Because she actually puts in the time and effort to dedicate her life to God. She sacrifices daily pleasures to devote time to serving the Lord–

ANA

And she makes a huge show of it.

NICOLASA

But she *does* it, Ana! Maybe if you spent less time ruminating on meaningless dreams—

ANA

Meaningless?

NICOLASA

I didn't mean that, I only—perhaps you could find meaning in things that are tangible, things that are quantifiable, like volunteering to lead the Rosary, like choosing to fast at meal time—

ANA

You really think my dreams are meaningless, Nica?

NICOLASA

I don't know! Maybe, maybe not! Not everything holds meaning, Ana. What holds meaning, in God's eyes at least, is obedience and work. There are expectations that come with choosing this life, and I need you to take it seriously, to take *me* seriously, instead of floating around in some fantasyland you've created.

ANA

Where is this coming from? Why do you all of a sudden have a problem with the way I view my faith—

NICOLASA

This is not about me. I told you things were going to have to be different around here. I've worked my entire life to get to where I am, Ana, I don't want to give the Bishop any reason not to trust me. So please, I am just asking you to change your routine, to be a little bit more disciplined–

ANA

I see God in everything I do, Nicolasa. I don't need to punish myself or fast until a state of exhaustion in an attempt to get closer to Him, because I see Him in every leaf on the orange trees, I see Him in the way the sun feels on my skin, I see Him in the love I feel for all the people around me. So, yes, I think my dreams hold meaning because I think *everything* holds meaning, it's not separate for me–

NICOLASA

(Firmly) Ana. I am telling you I need you to comply. You can adopt whatever la-la land inner philosophy you like, but you are a professed sister of the Monastery of Santa Catalina, and you must act accordingly. I am your Prioress, and you will do as I say. Do you understand?

ANA

(Through her teeth) Yes.

NICOLASA

This means you show up on time to your daily obligations, you *hold your tongue,* attend confession daily, not just when you feel like getting out of bed–I don't want to see you sitting around:

there's always something more you can be doing. People are watching us, Ana, and noticing. Do you understand?

ANA

Yes.

NICOLASA

Mass is starting soon. You should start the prelude.

ANA

Oh, am I already late for that too?

NICOLASA

I'm done, Ana. Do as I say, or there will be consequences.

(Nicolasa leaves her.)

SCENE 8

(In their bedroom, several weeks later. Ana is lying in bed already trying to fall asleep as Teresa enters.)

TERESA

Are you going to sleep already?

ANA

Yeah.

TERESA

Why?

ANA

I'm just tired. We have to get up early tomorrow.

TERESA

What is going on with you?

ANA

I just want to go to sleep early.

TERESA

You never want to go to sleep early. You're being *weird,* Ana, you have been for weeks, what's going on with you?

ANA

I'm just trying to "be better," "more disciplined." That's all.

TERESA

Why?

ANA

Because I want to!

TERESA

No you don't. You don't care about that stuff.

ANA

Maybe I changed my mind! Maybe I do now!

TERESA

You can't lie to me Ana, I know you too well.

(Beat.)

ANA

Nica told me I need to start caring more. I'm just trying to do what she wants.

TERESA

You? You care *so* much!

ANA

I guess not about the right things.

TERESA

I just don't understand, she's always been hard on you but she's never accused you of not *caring* before–

ANA

I guess it's that I don't care about being demonstrative and obedient. Which I don't. I am who I am, I don't care what people think of me, my relationship with God is *mine* and I know what brings me closer to him. Everything other than *that*–I don't care about.

TERESA

So why are you doing all this?

ANA

I have to. That's what she wants from me.

TERESA

You seem miserable.

ANA

Well I don't really have a choice, do I?

(Beat.)

Did you cut your hair?

TERESA

Yeah, earlier today.

ANA

It looks good. I like it.

TERESA

It was just getting too long to manage.

(Beat.)

ANA

It's kinda stupid, isn't it?

TERESA

What?

ANA

All the things Nicolasa wants me to do. Fast. Go to confession daily. "Hold my tongue." Make sure people see me praying conventionally. All the things that will somehow make God love me more.

TERESA

Confession is part of the catechism. And fasting.

ANA

But it's making me *miserable*! Isn't that a sign that something's wrong? Maybe not with the catechism itself but with the people enforcing it *now*, the expectations, the judgment. . . .

TERESA

You become the perfect Catholic for three weeks and you're already—

ANA

What is perfect? We're all perfect, we're all perfect in the eyes of God.

TERESA

Holy, then.

ANA

Holiness is relative. It has to be. I've been doing everything "right," and I've never felt less holy. I don't feel God at *all* anymore, Tere, and it terrifies me. . . .

TERESA

Well, God isn't a feeling, you can't rely on that. You just have to trust that He's there.

ANA

I just don't understand, since when do I have to be submissive and obedient and demonstrative in order to please God? Why does Nicolasa want that from me?

TERESA

I don't know. I don't think you do.

ANA

That's easy for you to say, it comes so naturally for you. There's just something wrong with *me* I guess, I'm just not good enough for Nicolasa anymore.

TERESA

That's not true.

ANA

Well *is* there something wrong with me? Or is there just something wrong with the Church? It's a bit arrogant to claim to know exactly what makes God happy, don't you think?

TERESA

The Fathers of our Church were divinely inspired—

ANA

And who's to say I can't be? Who's to say that any one person's way is better than someone else's? Just because they convinced more people to follow them?

TERESA

Maybe you do just need to go to bed. You're starting to sound a little blasphemous.

ANA

And then I think about all the things we said in our vows, all the promises we made, things we would never do, things that now, looking back, I can't even really understand the purpose of. I've just grown to accept it because I was told I had to in order to please God . . . but why?

TERESA

Are you questioning your vows?

ANA

No. I just—I was fourteen when I took mine. And I thought I was so old, so mature, but how fucked is it that I'm forever bound by a vow I made when I was fourteen? I hadn't even bled yet. That's a crazy choice to have to make.

TERESA

The beauty of the choice lies in its gravity.

ANA

How was I supposed to know who I was when I was fourteen? Did you?

TERESA

I don't know. No, not really. But I grow *with* God *within* my choice. I'm not afraid because he's with me every step of the way.

ANA

I've changed so much. I—I don't know. (A shift) Don't you ever *want* things? Things I thought I was perfectly content without when I was fourteen but then. . . . I don't know. I don't know.

TERESA

What?

ANA

Nothing.

TERESA

What is it?

ANA

Sometimes I just. . . . I don't know.

TERESA

I want things. Sometimes. Things I thought I wouldn't ever want if I just . . . forced myself not to.

(Beat.)

ANA

Like what?

(Beat. They look at each other.)

TERESA

Nothing. This is—never mind. We should really just go to bed. We shouldn't be talking about any of this.

(Teresa begins to undress. As she's taking her habit off, she turns around and sees Ana watching her. A moment of panic as she pulls her habit back up over her shoulder. They stare at each other for a moment and then, not breaking eye contact, Teresa lets her habit drop to the ground, leaving her in just her undergarments. She then pulls her nightgown on. They look at each other for a moment, not saying anything. Then, Ana stands up and does the same. She lets her hair down, lets her habit drop to the floor, and pulls her nightgown on over her head. They stand and take each other in.)

ANA

You're beautiful.

TERESA

(Worried) Ana . . .

ANA

I–

TERESA

Stop.

(Beat.)

ANA

I love you.

TERESA

How do you know?

ANA

I don't know.

TERESA

So maybe you don't.

ANA

I do. Do you?

TERESA

I don't know.

ANA

Yeah, you do.

TERESA

I do.

ANA

You do *know* or you do . . . *love*—

TERESA

No I do. . . . (she gestures to imply the latter option) I don't know.

(She sits down on her bed and covers her face with her hands.)

Stop. We should go to bed.

ANA

(Sitting down) Okay.

(Beat.)

TERESA

I do . . . love you . . . too. I think. I don't know.

ANA

That's okay.

(Beat.)

TERESA

Is this okay?

ANA

I don't know.

TERESA

Probably not.

ANA

(Smiling) Who's to say what God wants? This feels divinely inspired to me.

(Beat.)

TERESA

Your hair is . . . can I just—you always have so many tangles in it, can I . . . can I brush it for you?

ANA

You want to brush my hair?

TERESA

No. That was stupid.

(Ana stands up and walks over to Teresa's bed. She picks up the brush and puts it in Teresa's hand, sitting down next to her.)

ANA

Go ahead.

(Teresa looks out the window.)

There's no one there. It's fine.

(Teresa looks into Ana's eyes for a moment, then gently begins to brush her hair, face to face.)

TERESA

Turn around so I can. . . . I need to get the back. . . .

(Ana doesn't turn around. They look at each other for a tense moment, and then suddenly they are kissing. It is gentle and awkward and doesn't last very long. Teresa pulls away and stares at Ana. A moment passes.)

ANA

Is that okay? I'm sorry, I–

(Teresa goes back in and kisses Ana again, for a little bit longer this time. This time it's Ana that pulls away.)

ANA

One second.

(She goes to the window and thinks for a second, then grabs the habit she'd left on the floor and tries to figure out a way to get it to cover the window.)

ANA

Sorry I–(laughing) it won't stay. . . .

TERESA

(Grabbing her embroidery needles) Use these!

ANA

Use—what?

(Teresa comes over.)

TERESA

Hold it up.

(Ana positions the habit so it's covering the window. Teresa lines up the embroidery needle as though to pierce it into the wall through the habit, like a push pin.)

ANA

(Stopping her) Woah! Woah there, let's not destroy property now!

(Ana looks around and sees a broom leaning against the wall. She goes and grabs it and leans it against the window, bristle side down. She thinks, then flips it upside down so the handle is on the floor and the bristles are against the wall above the window. She then drapes the habit on top of the broom.)

ANA

There!

TERESA

The sides–

ANA

Shhhh!

(Ana grabs two books from Teresa's bed and uses them to prop up the sides of the habit so they cover the sides of the window.)

ANA

There. You satisfied?

(Teresa smiles, then grabs Ana's face and pulls her in for a kiss, longer and more passionate than the others. They migrate back towards Teresa's bed, getting back on the bed together, fumbling awkwardly with the mechanics of it. As they kiss, the light begins to shine bright white above. Ana does not notice.)

END ACT I.

ACT II

SCENE 9

(Ten years earlier. Ana rushes into the room she shares with Nicolasa, in a fit.)

ANA

Nica, they're so mean and I *hate* them!

NICOLASA

(Brushing her hair out of her face) Anita, what happened dear?

(Ana buries her face in Nicolasa's habit and screams.)

(Amused) Can you calm down and tell me what happened mijita?

ANA

They're *so* mean to Iwa.

NICOLASA

Who is?

ANA

The other girls. The younger servants. Some of the daughters.

NICOLASA

What happened? Why are you here and not working with the rest of them?

ANA

They sent me home. I yelled.

NICOLASA

Ana. . . . What does Jesus demonstrate for us when we're wronged? We turn the other cheek—

ANA

I can't Nica—I don't know *why* I get so angry but I just *do!* I want to be perfect like you tell me to be. I try. I really do try. I don't know what's wrong with me.

NICOLASA

(Pulling her in) Come here Ana.

(She begins taking out the pins in Ana's hair, which had been pulled up into a tight braided updo.)

It's not what we feel that matters, Anita. It's how we choose to act on those feelings. You are good. God made you perfectly.

ANA

But I just get so *mad*! Iwa was just trying her best, Nica. She's not as fast as the other girls and they always tease her for it and I just get so mad and I couldn't take it anymore!

NICOLASA

I think in some cases, anger is a sign of holiness.

ANA

What do you mean?

NICOLASA

We are not called by God to be complacent, mija. We are called to advocate for the poor, the hungry, those cast out by society—Jesus said to turn the other cheek, yes, but he also stormed into a temple being used by hypocrites, flipped over all the tables, and drove them all out. He was not a passive man, mija. I am very proud of you for standing up for Iwa.

ANA

Really?

NICOLASA

Absolutely.

ANA

But we always talk about my temper—

NICOLASA

I only worry that your temper will consume you, my love. You just have to know when it's righteous anger coming from God and when it's . . . not.

ANA

Sor Inés says anger is not ladylike.

NICOLASA

Sor Inés is seventy years old and often doesn't remember what she had for breakfast.

ANA

(Laughing) Nica!

NICOLASA

What? (Pulling Ana into a hug) Come here. You are good, mija. Don't worry about those girls. All you can do is stand up for Iwa and try to be a good example that they can follow.

ANA

Nica, what does God feel like to you?

NICOLASA

God isn't a feeling.

ANA

Well what is He?

NICOLASA

I don't know. He's God. He just is.

ANA

(The white light hums on above) When I pray, I feel God like a warm light in my heart, and in my belly. Like I just drank tea, or ate a really warm soup. And if I concentrate really hard, I can sometimes feel Him smile.

NICOLASA

You have such a beautiful mind, Anita. Some people say the Holy Spirit is the Love between the Father and the Son. The Father loved the Son so much, and the Son loved the Father so much in return, that their Love became tangible, became a spirit that is just as much God as either of them.

(She holds up her index finger to be the Father and Ana's index finger to be the Son, and interlocks them.)

ANA

So God is Love?

NICOLASA

I suppose, yes.

ANA

And then . . . is Love . . . God?

NICOLASA

You can look at it that way.

(Suddenly, the sound of a street band is faintly heard, as though it's right outside the walls. They both react to it.)

Ay dios mío. I thought I told them—Hey! Sorry, Anita. These strange men keep coming into our parlor and bringing their instruments. I've told them before, we don't want to hear it—un momentico, let me go take care of this.

(Nicolasa leaves. Ana sits on the bed and begins to listen to the music intently for a few moments. Just as a smile starts to spread on her face, we hear Nicolasa yelling at them outside.)

NICOLASA

Hey! Hey! Get out of here! Scram!

SCENE 10

(At breakfast. Ana and Teresa are mid conversation.)

ANA

You hated me when you first moved into my room.

TERESA

No I didn't.

ANA

You never spoke to me! You would just glare at me whenever I tried to say anything!

TERESA

You were messy—*are* messy. That's all. And I was shy.

ANA

Well that's why Nica put you with me, you know.

TERESA

What?

ANA

She got so mad at me one morning cause I slept through Mass, and when she came to find me my room was a disaster. Like it was really bad. She said the shame of living with someone else would force me to keep things clean.

TERESA

You never told me that!

ANA

And you were the perfect little student–she thought you could straighten me out.

TERESA

(playfully) No, you just made me worse.

ANA

I know, it really backfired on her, huh. You're such a heathen now.

TERESA

I was kidding!

ANA

I've *corrupted* you!

TERESA

No!

ANA

I've turned you into someone who (gasps dramatically) would embroider an *illegal heart* / on the sleeve of a habit!

TERESA

(Looking around in panic) Shhh!

ANA

A HEART!

TERESA

(Putting her hand over Ana's mouth) Shut up! I'm not *such* a Goody Two-shoes–

ANA

Don't you remember the time–

TERESA

No, stop, I already know what you're going to say–

ANA

When Sor Luisa gave you two pieces of cake because she was being nice–

(They're both laughing so hard it's hard to breathe.)

TERESA

Stop–

ANA

She winked at you and everything–

TERESA

(Laughing) I can't breathe–

ANA

–and you TOLD ON HER?!

TERESA

I didn't mean to–

ANA

You didn't mean to?

TERESA

No, I mean I didn't mean to get her in trouble–

(As they're laughing, María walks up and sits with them.)

MARÍA

What's so funny?

TERESA

It's a long story.

MARÍA

I have time.

ANA

No, it's—you really had to be there.

MARÍA

You two are in an awfully good mood today.

ANA

What do you mean? We're always in good moods. We're just cheery spirits.

(Teresa chokes on her water.)

MARÍA

Okay. My morning was good. Although Tesa, I spoke to my father in the rejas last night.

TERESA

(Suddenly more serious) Last night? But you spoke to him last month.

MARÍA

No I didn't.

TERESA

Oh. I swore you did.

MARÍA

Anyway, they found Luisa. (She gets a blank stare from Ana and Teresa) Luisa la Roja, the one who ran away?

TERESA

Oh! How is she? Is she okay?

MARÍA

She was two cities away, sharing a bed with her dresser. The rumors were true, everything people were saying about her. Isn't that crazy?

ANA

Can we not talk about this?

MARÍA

Why?

ANA

I don't feel like gossiping about someone I don't know, especially about something like that. (Getting up to go) I'm going to get more beans. (She goes.)

MARÍA

What is her deal? You'd think I insulted a family member or something. She doesn't even know Luisa.

TERESA

I'm gonna go check on her, actually.

MARÍA

Okay.

(Teresa follows Ana into the kitchen, where they're alone.)

TERESA

Hey, are you alright? I know how María gets to you—

(Ana cuts her off with a kiss. Teresa pulls away, nervous.)

Stop it, someone could see.

ANA

Why would they suspect anything? We're always alone together. No one would think to check.

(Ana kisses her again quickly.)

TERESA

María would.

ANA

María's too busy saying her seventieth Rosary this morning.

TERESA

We should be more careful.

ANA

Fine. You're right. (Kissing her again) Just one more—

TERESA

(Smiling as she pulls away) Ana!

ANA

What? After breakfast I'm not gonna see you until dinner time at least, I needed something to hold me over!

TERESA

(Taunting her as she leaves) Okay, you're fine, I'm going back!

ANA

No, come back! (Ana chases her offstage.)

SCENE 11

(Just before Mass. Ana walks in and sees María at the cantor stand, organizing music and getting ready. A few nuns have started to fill the pews, but it's mostly empty.)

ANA

What's this? What are you doing?

MARÍA

Oh, did the Prioress not tell you? I'm singing at Mass today.

(Beat.)

ANA

No, she did not tell me.

MARÍA

Oh. That's weird. I'm sorry, I didn't mean to make things awkward, I assumed you knew. . . .

ANA

Well, I didn't.

MARÍA

I really didn't—

ANA

Where is she?

MARÍA

Who? The—

ANA

Madre Nicolasa.

MARÍA

I think she's over there talking to Padre—

ANA

Thanks. (She starts to leave, then turns around. As genuinely as she can muster:) Good luck. It's really scary the first few times, but you'll be great.

MARÍA

(Surprised) Thank you.

ANA

Yeah.

(She looks at her for a moment, then turns around to go find Nicolasa. She intercepts her as she's walking.)

Nica, what's going on?

NICOLASA

Ana—can it wait? I have things I need to attend to—

ANA

Why is María singing?

NICOLASA

Ana, take a seat, we'll talk about it later—

ANA

Why wouldn't you at least warn me?

NICOLASA

It was a last minute decision. Don't blame María—

ANA

You only care about María's feelings? Even now you're trying to protect her, spare her from my wrath?

NICOLASA

I just know how you are with her—

ANA

I don't care about María—I'm asking you: why? I've been better! I've been doing *everything* you tell me to do! I've been showing up early, I've been going above and beyond, I've been quiet, I didn't say a single cruel word to María just now, I even told her *good luck* and gave her advice—

NICOLASA

Ana. Maybe this has nothing to do with you. Maybe I just wanted to give María a chance because she has proven herself time and time again—

ANA

And I haven't?

NICOLASA

It has nothing to do with you, Ana! You are an excellent singer. You do this well. But María does, too, and she deserves a chance to—

ANA

What, you think she does it better than me? I've heard her sing, Nica, I know that's not true.

NICOLASA

(Firmly) Sor Ana. I am done with this conversation.

ANA

I just don't understand! I've been doing everything right, Nica—

NICOLASA

If you want to have this conversation, come outside. I'm not going to make a scene in front of the other sisters. They're trying to pray, to prepare themselves for Mass.

ANA

Fine. Let's go outside.

(They walk out the back door together.)

ANA

Is there something wrong with the way I've been singing lately? Why are you taking this away from me?

NICOLASA

For the last time, Ana, this is not about you.

ANA

I don't believe you.

NICOLASA

Do you want the truth? No, you're not performing like you used to. You sound lifeless.

ANA

Because I'm burnt out, Nica! Because I'm bending over backwards trying to do everything you're telling me to do—

NICOLASA

(Cutting her off) But that is not the reason I let María sing today. The Bishop requested it. It was beyond my power. I still believe in you as a singer, Ana, you have a special gift, and I know you will find your way back to it, but maybe María could have that too. She deserves the right to find out.

ANA

This is the one thing I had.

NICOLASA

This is not a personal attack, Ana.

ANA

It feels like one! Suddenly nothing I do is ever good enough for you! What changed? Why is it *impossible* to please you, Nica?!

NICOLASA

Madre Nicolasa.

ANA

Madre Nicolasa.

NICOLASA

You're putting me in an impossible situation, Ana. Is it so much to ask for you to treat me with the respect I deserve?

ANA

I don't understand what more you want from me.

NICOLASA

I'm going back inside. We can continue this discussion later if you want.

ANA

No. I don't want to.

NICOLASA

Fine. I tried my best.

(Nicolasa leaves. Ana sits on the curb in front of the door. After a moment, Teresa comes out of the back door and finds her.)

TERESA

(Confused) Hey, what's going on, what happened? María said you came out here.

ANA

Everything's always about María.

TERESA

All I said was she told me you came out here.

ANA

And didn't you see where she said it from?

TERESA

I did, was that not your choice? I assumed Madre Nicolasa would have talked to you about it.

ANA

She did not.

TERESA

Oh no.

ANA

Did you know this was happening? Did María talk to you about it?

TERESA

No, I didn't. But hey, this could be good! It's less work on your plate.

ANA

She's not even good!

TERESA

She has a very pretty voice.

ANA

(Sarcastically) Hm.

TERESA

Are you mad at me?

ANA

No.

TERESA

I'm just saying that it doesn't need to be the end of the world. It's just Mass. Who cares?

ANA

I said I wasn't mad at you!

TERESA

Fine.

ANA

It's not "just Mass," it's—it's so much more than that.

TERESA

(Empathetically) How?

ANA

It just is.

TERESA

Maybe it isn't.

ANA

It *is.*

(Beat.)

The singer worships God with their voice. That's the one thing I can do.

TERESA

So can María. It will still be a prayerful Mass.

ANA

Why do you like her? You don't see her problem?

TERESA

We're all flawed and we're all just trying our best, Ana.

ANA

You really do just see the best in everyone. Ugh! Even when I'm mad at you I can't even be mad at you because you're so—

TERESA

I thought you said you weren't mad at me.

ANA

I'm not!

TERESA

So what's the problem? Can we go back inside? I don't want to walk in once it's already started.

(She sits down next to her and grabs her hand.)

Talk to me, Ana.

ANA

Just—nothing feels the way it did before. I—I don't know how to explain it. And this was the one thing I still had. Maybe Nicolasa hates me, maybe I'm questioning everything, maybe I feel like a sinner every time I *look* at you, but I still had *this*. I could still do this *one thing* and feel like maybe God doesn't hate me, too. Like, if I can still help other people connect with God, maybe it doesn't matter what I feel or what I do, you know? I'll know I'm doing something right.

TERESA

Is this . . . am *I* drawing you away from God?

ANA

No—no! That's not what I meant at all—you're the best thing that's ever happened to me and I know in my heart that God meant for us to find each other. I know it. (Grabbing her face) Look at me, I promise you. I know it. I just . . . don't think Nicolasa would feel the same. And for me. . . .

TERESA

I know.

ANA

It's sometimes hard to separate God's voice from hers.

TERESA

Yeah.

ANA

I miss her, Tere.

TERESA

I know.

(Beat.)

ANA

I don't want to go back in there. I don't want to watch María sing. I don't want to see Nicolasa.

TERESA

Come in and sit with me. You don't even have to look at her.

(Ana says nothing. Teresa grabs her face and turns it towards her.)

Come on, come to Mass with me. We've never sat with each other at Mass before 'cause you're always singing, it'll be fun.

ANA

(Smiling) Yeah, okay.

(The door opens wider behind them. María starts to come outside just as Teresa leans in and kisses Ana gently. María's eyes widen and she quickly recedes back into the church. Ana and Teresa do not notice.)

Wow, bold of you.

TERESA

I wanted to. (Standing and helping Ana up) Okay, let's go.

ANA

Let's.

(As they stand, María walks outside as though it was her first time.)

María?

MARÍA

(Genuinely) Hi, I—I was just checking on you. I really am sorry, I didn't know she hadn't told you. I don't have to sing today, you can sing, I feel so bad for—

ANA

(Genuinely) No, no. It's not your fault. I'm not mad at you. Please, sing. I meant what I said earlier, you're gonna do great. (She smiles) I can't wait to hear it.

MARÍA

Thank you. It means a lot, coming from you.

ANA

Thanks for checking on me.

MARÍA

Of course. I should get back, just wanted to–

ANA

Yeah. Go, before the Prioress gets mad at you too. Sorry, bad joke?

MARÍA

(Smiling) It's fine, I won't tell her.

(As María leaves, Teresa squeezes Ana's hand.)

TERESA

Well *that* was really good.

ANA

(Shrugging) You make me better, I guess. Alright, let's go.

(They walk into the church together, dropping hands as they enter the threshold.)

SCENE 12

(The roof at night. Ana and Teresa come up the stairs, hand in hand.)

TERESA

This never gets old.

ANA

I know.

TERESA

I feel so. . . .

ANA

What?

TERESA

I just . . . feel so many things now. Recently. I didn't know I could feel so many things.

ANA

Like what?

TERESA

Right now, awe. At the world. At you. Everything in my life had been so safe, so contained, and you've expanded it all for me.

ANA

You too, for me.

TERESA

Really?

ANA

Yeah.

TERESA

Do you think we're disappointing God?

ANA

(Certain) No. I can't imagine a God that does not want us to be together.

TERESA

Do you think I'm disappointing my younger self?

(Beat.)

ANA

Is that how you feel?

TERESA

No. Yes. I don't know. (More sure of herself) No. I'm not. Disappointing her, I mean. Myself.

(Ana looks at her.)

She used to—*I* used to dream about love. Fantasize that one day I'd . . . I don't know. . . . I didn't really know what being in love was, I guess, but younger me wanted it so bad. And then when I came here I grieved that she would—that *I* would never have that. Anyway, the point is that I don't think she's disappointed, that was a stupid thought. If anything, this—all of this—sure I'm breaking the rules, sure I'm not exactly being a perfect nun (Ana laughs), but this is making me feel closer to her—to who I am—than I've felt in years.

ANA

I love you.

TERESA

(Smiling) Do you really?

ANA

Shut up. Yes, I do.

(They look out at the city together.)

Do you feel . . . scared?

TERESA

Yeah. Do you?

(Ana nods.)

ANA

Do you feel angry?

TERESA

Do you?

ANA

I have these moments when I'm with you and I forget everything else in the world exists, and all there is is you and me and this roof and right now, and for just a second everything makes sense and I don't feel the world closing in on me. But then I think about how I can never marry you. I think about how I can never kiss you in public, or yell from the rooftops how much I love you. You deserve to be yelled from the rooftops, Teresa.

TERESA

I don't want to talk about this right now.

ANA

Sorry.

TERESA

I know it's stupid, but I just. . . . I just want to pretend. (Ana looks at her) Can we be more than just what we cannot be? For a moment?

(Beat.)

ANA

(Pointing) That one's ours.

TERESA

What?

ANA

That's our house. Way over there. The one with the clay rooftop.

TERESA

They *all* have clay /rooftops.

ANA

That one! Right there! Just left of the plaza. (Taking her hand and pointing with it) See the corner of the plaza? Now walk down that street, take a left. Second house on the right. With the chimney on the right side.

TERESA

Okay yes I see it–

ANA

That one's ours.

TERESA

What are you talking about?

ANA

(Moving her finger down) We got married there. That church. Everyone we know came. Your dad gave you away.

TERESA

(Catching on) Ana . . .

ANA

Oh, did you pick up fish from the market on the way home? I need it for dinner tonight.

TERESA

(Smiling) What?

ANA

I said I needed fish. Didn't you go to the market on your way home?

TERESA

(Deciding to play along) You didn't tell me you were making dinner tonight. What are you making?

ANA

Ceviche.

TERESA

Oh. Well no, I did not go to the market. Was I supposed to?

ANA

Teresa! It's a Thursday, I *always* make dinner on Thursdays.

TERESA

It's Sunday.

ANA

No, it's *Thursday*.

TERESA

Oh, right. How could I forget our Thursday dinners?
I must have gotten distracted, there was a beautiful girl singing with her band in the plaza today . . .

ANA

Oh, was there?

TERESA

That's how we met, actually. I'd always hear you singing in the plaza, and I just fell in love with your voice. One day you finally confronted me for staring at you all those weeks.

ANA

I'd been staring at you, too. I was too nervous to say anything.

TERESA

Oh, were you now?

ANA

But now you're my muse, I write all my songs about you.

TERESA

(Getting an idea) Can we have a kid?

ANA

(Suddenly serious) You want kids?

(She shrugs.)

TERESA

It's just make believe.

(Beat.)

ANA

How many kids do we have?

TERESA

Just one. A boy.

ANA

He starts school tomorrow! We've gotta get him ready!

TERESA

(Getting more excited) I'll make sure he has all his supplies, can you pack him some food for tomorrow morning?

ANA

Hang on, what's his name?

TERESA

Baltasar.

(Their lines begin to overlap.)

ANA

Baltasar? Really? Of all the names in the world you go with Baltasar? Not /Carlos or Diego or–

TERESA

(Laughing) Just pack *Baltasar Gonzalo de Salinas's* /lunch–

ANA

/Oh, is that his full legal name?

TERESA

–he likes pork humitas with boiled potatoes and a banana–

ANA

/Jeez, Baltasar has some awful taste.

TERESA

Shut up! Just–agh!

ANA

Okay, okay, I'll slave away in the kitchen cooking Balty's food. Anything else?

TERESA

My father wanted us to come by tomorrow to take a look at his will, are you free?

ANA

His will?

TERESA

We need to take a look at which of his assets /he's leaving for us and which are going to my sisters–

ANA

Okay I'm hiring someone who's doing all of this for us, his name is Baltasar Guava y Queso de Salty Niñas Sr. /We named our son after him.

TERESA

/Gonzalo de Salinas!

ANA

Actually we don't even need your father's money 'cause I'm super rich. We found out that my family is actually minor Spanish royalty, and we don't even live here anymore, we just spend all of our time traveling the world.

TERESA

After Baltasar gets married.

ANA

After Baltasar gets married, of course.

TERESA

Baltasar needs a stable place to grow up, we can't just upend his life like that–

ANA

Which one? The one I hired to help with /your father's will?

TERESA

The one who's our son.

ANA

Oh right. The other Baltasar realizes his profession is a joke and runs away with a seamstress named Claudia.

TERESA

Hm. I hope he's happy.

ANA

We're dining with the elite in France, what do we care?

(They laugh gently. Beat.)

TERESA

(Nestles into her deeper) There's so much I . . .

ANA

I know.

TERESA

That I wish.

ANA

I like to think that there's another universe where we just argue about what to eat for dinner that night. And none of the rest of this matters. If we can't have that life, I like to think that somewhere, another version of us can.

TERESA

I hope they're happy. You and me.

ANA

Yeah. Me too.

(Suddenly, the sound of instrumental music is faintly heard.)

Shhh! Shh! Do you hear that? Listen!

TERESA

Just barely.

ANA

I love it when they do that. This is the only place in the convent where you can hear them.

(Beat.)

TERESA

You deserve to be shouted from the rooftops, too.

ANA

(Pulling her in) Let's just listen to the music and pretend.

TERESA

Okay.

(They hold each other and listen to the music, playing with each other's fingers, feeling the curves of each others' hands. They interlock index fingers.)

SCENE 13

(Nicolasa's office. Nicolasa sits at her desk, distressed. Ana knocks on the door.)

NICOLASA

Come in.

ANA

You wanted to see me?

NICOLASA

Sit down.

(Ana does. Nicolasa says nothing.)

ANA

What is it? Is this about you wanting María to sing more?

NICOLASA

No, this is not about Sor María.

ANA

So what is it?

(Silence.)

NICOLASA

Something has been brought to my attention recently that I must address with you. Actions have already been taken to . . . prevent further damage, but the question remains of what to do . . . with you, from here.

ANA

(Concerned) What are you talking about?

NICOLASA

I think you know, Sor Ana.

ANA

No, I—I don't know what you're talking about.

(Beat.)

NICOLASA

You and Sor Teresa. Your . . . relationship.

(Silence.)

ANA

What?

NICOLASA

Don't play dumb, Ana. Sor Teresa already admitted to everything. María revealed to me that she had seen the two of you . . . kissing. We brought Teresa in, questioned her. She told us everything.

ANA

Us? You allowed María to be a part of that conversation?

NICOLASA

Stop putting words in my mouth.

ANA

Why would you speak to Teresa first? What, you knew you had more control over her? You could get her to confess easier?

NICOLASA

Ana–

ANA

How did she take it? Where is she now? Is she okay?

NICOLASA

We're not here to talk about Sor Teresa, we're here to talk about you.

(Beat.)

ANA

You said actions had already been taken to prevent further damage. What did you do?

(Nicolasa says nothing.)

(Firmer) What did you do?

NICOLASA

Sor Teresa is being transferred to a convent in Mexico.

(Ana sits silent for a moment, then stands up quickly and heads to the door.)

ANA

Where is she now—

NICOLASA

Sor Ana! Sit down. Sor Teresa is still here. But like I said, we are not here to talk about Sor Teresa. We're here to talk about you.

ANA

I love her, Nica.

(Beat.)

NICOLASA

You will remain at Santa Catalina so I can keep a close eye on you. You will take a hiatus from your duties as the monastery musician until we've determined that you have adequately repented and restored your relationship with God—

ANA

You know nothing about my relationship with God—

NICOLASA

In the meantime, María will take over as lead musician and cantor.

(Beat.)

ANA

You just had to include that part, just had to drive the knife in one last time.

NICOLASA

It's the most logical solution, Ana.

ANA

And you and María both win! Go ahead, give her everything she wants! How convenient, she sells us out and gets to take everything she's wanted since she got here.

NICOLASA

For the last time Sor Ana, this is not about María!

ANA

I'm sure you're just thrilled about this new arrangement. You've been wanting to replace me with María since she got here. In every way possible.

NICOLASA

(Pleading) Why do you think the absolute worst of me, Ana? I am trying to do everything right, trying to please the Bishop, trying to protect you, I don't know what you expect me to do! Why do you *hate* me? What did I do wrong, where did I fail you?

ANA

I don't hate you, I've never said I hated you, I just needed so much from you—

NICOLASA

I gave you what you needed! I gave you God, I taught you music, I taught you law and truth, I made you Holy—

ANA

I needed *love,* Nica!

NICOLASA

You're not my daughter.

(Beat.)

ANA

You're right. I'm not.

NICOLASA

Ana—

ANA

(Coldly, mockingly) I apologize, Reverenda Madre Nicolasa Inés de Jesús, for my insolence. (Standing) Please, may I have leave to go back to my cell?

NICOLASA

Ana stop it—

ANA

You brought me in here like it was gonna be a discussion, but you just decided exactly what you were going to do with us before you even spoke to me. You didn't think for a second that you might owe me more than that?

NICOLASA

I had to make decisions as Prioress.

ANA

Right. (Walking to the door) Do you permit me to leave, Prioress?

(Beat.)

NICOLASA

If you have nothing else to say to me, you may leave.

ANA

Do you have anything more you want to say to me? Any last jabs?

NICOLASA

Just leave, Ana. I'm done being berated by you. I've only ever tried to protect you—I hope you know that. You are responsible for your own actions and for everything that happens to you and Sor Teresa from here on out.

(Beat.)

ANA

Fine.

(She leaves. Nicolasa is left alone.)

SCENE 14

(Ana and Teresa's room. Teresa is packing all her things into a bag. Ana enters. They look at each other for a moment, not saying anything. Then—)

TERESA

María told Nicolasa.

ANA

I know.

TERESA

So. . . .

ANA

Yeah.

TERESA

Was this all a mistake, Ana?

ANA

I don't know.

TERESA

Me neither.

ANA

I don't think it was.

TERESA

Well they're not sending you to Mexico.

ANA

I'm sorry.

(Beat.)

TERESA

I don't know how I could have been so stupid.

ANA

You chose to *love,* Tere. That could never be stupid.

TERESA

Are you kidding? Even if it didn't go against everything the church has ever taught us, we took permanent vows of chastity, Ana!

ANA

So we can't love because why? Because whoever the hell my birth mother was decided to leave me on the steps of a convent? Because you happened to be born the youngest daughter of a family who couldn't afford another dowry? We didn't choose this life, you were forced into it almost as much as I was—

TERESA

We chose to take the vows, we knew what it meant, and we broke them! We deserve this—

ANA

Even if the vows are fucking stupid? How was I supposed to know I'd fall in love?

TERESA

You don't, that's the point! When you profess, you make a conscious choice to sacrifice your life for God!

ANA

You can't truly believe that God didn't want this for us. I refuse to believe that this was a sin, that anything about this was going against God's will because I *know* Him, I've known Him my whole life, and I've never felt closer to Him than when I'm with you.

TERESA

That's not the point. We broke the rules intentionally, and now we're facing the consequences of our actions. It's over. There's nothing we can do.

ANA

What if we left?

(Beat.)

TERESA

What?

ANA

What if we left? Together? Like Luisa la Roja and her dresser. Moved somewhere new, pretended we were sisters . . . we could have that house with the clay roof and make dinner on Thursdays.

TERESA

No . . . we can't do that.

ANA

Why not?

TERESA

Could we do that?

ANA

Come with me. We'll leave tonight. You're already packed.

(Beat.)

TERESA

No, I—I'm not like you, Ana. I can't just . . . no.

ANA

Why?

TERESA

Because! Because—because I can't! Because I'm going to Mexico.

ANA

You don't want to go to Mexico.

TERESA

Yeah, no shit I don't want to go! You get to stay. Your life will just go back to the way it was before I got here. I have to leave everything I've ever known.

ANA

Stop being a coward.

TERESA

(Hurt) I'm not a coward, Ana. I made a vow that I would live a life in complete devotion to God. And when I took that vow, I meant it. God is everything to me. And I thought I could have both, I thought I could . . . have love *and* Love—

ANA

You can have both. Why can't we have both?

TERESA

I wish we could have both, Ana. I do. You have helped me grow closer to God than I could have ever imagined because in loving you, I finally understand a fraction of the love He must have for me. And I will always be thankful to you for teaching me what Love is. But I can't leave with you because I choose Him.

ANA

Well not me, I choose *you,* I'll always choose you–

TERESA

Please don't make this harder than it has to be, Ana.

ANA

I just don't understand–

TERESA

Please, Ana.

ANA

But I'll never see you again. Ever.

(Beat.)

TERESA

I know.

ANA

You'll never see your family again.

TERESA

(Smiling through pain) It's all part of the sacrifice. I'll find new people . . . in Mexico.

ANA

You're hard set on this?

TERESA

Yes.

(Beat.)

ANA

Then you're not going to Mexico. I'm not gonna let them send you to Mexico.

TERESA

What?

ANA

(Standing up) I'm going to go talk to Nicolasa. You're not going to Mexico.

TERESA

What are you talking about?

ANA

Just trust me.

(She starts to leave, then turns around.)

Just . . . think about it. Going together. I know. . . .I know how you feel, but please. Just think about it. Promise me?

(Beat.)

TERESA

Okay. I will.

(Ana leaves.)

SCENE 15

(Nicolasa's office. Nicolasa is right where Ana left her. Ana bursts in.)

ANA

I want to leave.

NICOLASA

What?

ANA

Teresa can stay, I'll leave.

NICOLASA

You can't go to Mexico in her place, we need you here.

ANA

Not Mexico. I don't want to be a nun anymore. I want to leave.

(Beat.)

NICOLASA

You can't leave, you have nowhere to go–

ANA

Write to the Bishop. Get me permission to leave. This is her home.

NICOLASA

You have no one! You have no family, you have no money–

ANA

If you don't write to the Bishop, I will pack my bags and walk out in the middle of the night.

NICOLASA

You would be excommunicated. You would go to Hell.

ANA

I'm leaving. Tomorrow. Whether or not you choose to nullify my vows. (She starts to leave)

NICOLASA

(An act of desperation) Ana wait, please! Stop, just–can we talk about this, for a second? Don't make a rash decision you'll regret.

ANA

I had a dream a few weeks ago. I didn't tell you about it . . . for obvious reasons.

NICOLASA

Ana. . . .

ANA

I had a dream that I was at the funeral for an old man. I didn't know who he was, but there were so many people there to celebrate his life, and they all got up one by one and told stories about all the things he did . . . and like, what will I leave behind when I'm gone? What will my funeral look like? Maybe a few sisters telling stories about my voice? I'm more than that, Nica. I want to be more than that. Don't I owe it to Him to become everything I'm meant to be?

NICOLASA

You made a promise to God to give up your life in service. Do not take that lightly.

ANA

I don't think God meant for me to live like this! I want to get to know God by getting to know His creations. He made every detail of our world, He created my humanity, why would He want me to lock myself up and repress every feeling? I cannot be fully human in the way that God intended me to be until I face each part of my humanity head-on: otherwise what will I have to show for myself when I finally go to Him?

NICOLASA

No. I forbid you to leave. I won't give you permission. If you leave, you will be damning yourself.

ANA

Nica, please.

NICOLASA

Do you realize how lucky you are to be here, Ana? No, I will not let you leave because you need to learn the value of a promise. You can't go about making promises to God that you decide you want to break on a whim—

ANA

I professed when I was *fourteen,* Nica! I didn't know who I was! I had never experienced anything other than you and God and the monastery, and so of course that's what I thought I wanted! But I was a kid!

NICOLASA

(A last ditch desperate attempt) A vow is a vow, Ana. It would do you good to remember some fear of the Lord. Our God is an angry, wrathful God. The God of Sodom and Gomorrah, the God who sends floods and plagues and throws souls into lakes of fire. We do what we do so we can be rewarded with eternal life. This isn't some game!

ANA

I prefer the God who came to Earth as a slave, who kissed lepers and held company with prostitutes, and didn't care who you were or what you did as long as you did it with love.

NICOLASA

He still cared about sin, Ana.

ANA

What we did was not a sin!

NICOLASA

What are you talking about?

ANA

God made me like this, and He made me perfectly! Are you gonna tell me He made a mistake? That He made me so that my very existence was sinful?

NICOLASA

You didn't have to fall in love with Teresa, Ana. Your existence isn't sinful, your choices were.

ANA

What kind of a God would do that? Would create me with the ability to love and the desire to love but trick me and say, (wagging her finger) "Ah ah ah! If you do it, you'll be sinning against me!" That's not the God *you* taught me about.

NICOLASA

I clearly didn't teach you a *lot* of things.

ANA

I'm leaving tomorrow. With or without your permission. Whether you decide to nullify my vows or not.

NICOLASA

I will not. And you do not have my permission.

(Beat.)

ANA

Is the only reason you don't want me to go because of the principle of the matter? Because it's against the rules? No other reason?

(Silence.)

NICOLASA

Yes.

(Beat. Ana stands up and walks to the door.)

ANA

I'm sorry I couldn't be the daughter you wanted me to be. I wish I could've been, too.

(They look at each other for a moment. Nicolasa opens her mouth to say something, then closes it. Ana leaves.)

SCENE 16

(Dawn the next day, at the front gates of the monastery. Ana stands with her bags like a groom at the altar, waiting for Teresa. Suddenly, she comes running around the corner, holding a letter.)

TERESA

(Angrily) Are you stupid? You're actually going to leave?

ANA

Come with me, please.

TERESA

You can't just *leave!* Especially not for a stupid reason like trying to save me from Mexico—

ANA

I can, and I will.

TERESA

You're going regardless, even if I don't come?

ANA

I'll wait for you Tere, you can go get your bags.

(Teresa says nothing for a long moment, she just looks at Ana.)

ANA

It's okay. I understand.

TERESA

I'm sorry.

ANA

I know.

TERESA

Do you hate me?

ANA

I could never hate you.

TERESA

But you do.

ANA

I don't.

TERESA

(About to cry) I think I might hate *you*.

(They look at each other. Ana pulls her into a hug. María enters tentatively, holding a sealed envelope.)

MARÍA

Hi . . . I know you probably don't want to see me right now—

ANA

We don't.

MARÍA

(Genuine) I'm sorry.

TERESA

What do you want, María?

MARÍA

(Handing Ana the envelope) Nicolasa wanted me to give this to you.

ANA

What is it?

MARÍA

I don't know. She wouldn't tell me.

(Ana looks at the envelope for a moment.)

MARÍA

You don't have to believe me, but I really am sorry. I didn't want any of this.

ANA

Then you shouldn't have done it.

(Beat.)

MARÍA

I loved David. I wanted to marry him, and I would've, but my father made me come here as a favor to the Bishop. All my life I've been perfect and obedient, and this is what it got me.

TERESA

Why did you lie?

MARÍA

I don't know.

ANA

Why are you telling us now?

MARÍA

I don't know. Just—I'm sorry. I don't even control my own life. I didn't have a choice. I hope you can forgive me. (She goes.)

ANA

(To Teresa) Don't let her make your life a living hell.

TERESA

I know her secret now. She won't tell mine. (Gesturing to the envelope) What is it?

(Ana opens the envelope and gently unfolds a piece of paper. She stares at it for a long moment, unreadable.)

ANA

Nica nullified my vows.

TERESA

She did? What else did she say?

ANA

It's not a letter, it's just the certificate.

(They say nothing for a long moment.)

I guess she's not coming to say goodbye.

TERESA

She's letting you leave, though, isn't she? That's a lot for her.

ANA

But she's not going to say goodbye.

(A long beat. Ana wipes a tear, then takes a deep breath.)

Well! No more Sor Ana Cecelia, I am just Ana now. There is officially nothing stopping me from walking out those gates right now.

(Beat. They look at each other.)

Do you ever notice how we always tell children the truth about God? The pure, innocent truth? And then once we grow up, people try to twist the idea of Him into something cruel and vindictive?

TERESA

Yeah.

ANA

I don't know why I'm thinking about that. Nica, I guess. I wonder if she ever prays to the God she taught me about when I was a kid anymore.

TERESA

That's the God I believe in.

ANA

Me too.

TERESA

(Smiling) Are you just gonna walk out there in your habit?

ANA

I only brought this one. (Gesturing to her bags) The rest of it is just undergarments and nightgowns. But I wanted to keep this one. 'Cause look . . .

(She shows Teresa the inside of her sleeve. A little embroidered heart. They smile at each other.)

(Taking a sharp inhale) Okay. (She picks up her bags) I guess it's time.

TERESA

I guess so.

(They look at each other for a moment, then Teresa goes to Ana and holds her, both of them clinging to each other as if they are taking their last breath. After a long moment that would never be quite long enough, Teresa pulls away.)

I have to go . . . get to the Rosary.

ANA

Right.

TERESA

I'll listen for you on the roof. Sing loud for me.

(She starts to walk away, then turns back.)

Thank you, Ana. For everything.

(They look at each other for a moment, then Teresa goes. Ana smiles as she picks up her bags again. She turns around towards the gate and takes a deep breath. As she opens it, the white light hums on above her and burns brighter than it ever has before. She looks up at it and basks in it for a moment before stepping out into the street and walking off into her life.)

END.